# UNMOVED

## A Passionate Plea to the Listless Church in America

Josiah D. Martin

**UNMOVED**

A Passionate Plea to the Listless Church in America

Published by Total Fusion Press
6475 Cherry Run Rd. Strasburg, OH 44680
www.totalfusionpress.com



ISBN-10: 1-943496-00-5
ISBN-13: 978-1-943496-00-6

Library of Congress Control Number: 2015942689

Scriptures are taken from the KING JAMES VERSION (KJV): KING JAMES VERSION, public domain.

Edited by : Aimie Ladrach

Published in association with Total Fusion Ministries, Strasburg, OH. www.totalfusionministries.org

# CONTENTS

# ACKNOWLEDGMENTS

I wish to personally thank the following people for their contribution, encouragement, and knowledge that so greatly helped in creating this book:

First, I want to offer my thanks to my dear wife and partner in the ministry, Amy, who enthusiastically supports all of my new projects with undying love and devotion.

I would like to thank my parent, Pastor Rob and Kelly Martin, my brother Josh and my sister Rachel. along with the many brothers and sisters in Christ who have helped to encourage my walk with God.

My grateful appreciation to my friends, fellow soldiers in the faith, and editors Terry and Aimie Ladrach, who gave their very best to make this book all that it could be.

To the men of God who have over the years so deeply invested in my ministry and life, I offer my deepest gratitude; Allen Combs, Tim Finkey, David King, and Rob Martin, just to name a few.

I would like to recognize with gratitude the countless preachers and martyrs who faithfully stood in the face of fierce opposition and regardless of the cost, did all they could to preserve our Godly heritage.

Most of all I would like to thank my Savior Jesus Christ, who is my purpose and passion in life—the one to whom I owe my heart, my love, my life, and my all.

# A Prayer for Revival

"O God, send us the Holy Ghost! Give us both the breath of spiritual life and the fire of unconquerable zeal! O Thou who art our God, answer us both by wind and fire, and then we shall see Thee to be God indeed. The kingdom comes not, and the work is flagging. Oh, that Thou wouldst send the wind and the fire! Thou wilt do this when we are all of one accord, all believing, all expecting, all prepared by prayer. Lord, bring us to this waiting state! God, send us a season of glorious disorder. Oh, for a sweep of the wind that will set the seas in motion, and make our ironclad brethren, now lying so quietly at anchor, to roll from stem to stem. Oh, for the fire to fall again-fire which shall affect the most stolid! Oh, that such fire might first sit upon the disciples and then fall all around! O God, Thou art ready to work with us today even as Thou didst then. Stay not, we beseech Thee, but work at once. Break down every barrier that hinders the incoming of Thy might! Give us both hearts of flame and tongues of fire to preach Thy reconciling Word, for Jesus' sake! Amen!"

**– Charles H. Spurgeon**

# CHAPTER 1

## The "Numbed-Down" American Church

*"The world has lost the power to blush over its vice; the Church has lost her power to weep over it."* - Leonard Ravenhill

Throughout my years of ministry, I've had the privilege of meeting a great number of Christians from all walks of life. The good folks comprising the body of Christ across America are culturally diverse not only in their doctrinal beliefs, but also in their styles of worship, service roles, and their Christian experience in general. Included among them were countless individuals who had spent their entire lives in the house of God as well as those who had begun attending church shortly before or just after their salvation experience.

Despite the overwhelming claims by those who profess to be followers of Christ and express a desire to see lost souls saved, I've observed a disturbing thread that appears to run throughout the fabric of the contemporary church in America.

If you were to ask me to describe the average church in a single word, that word would have to be "unmoved." Oh, don't get me wrong; there is no lack of adherence to tradition. Professing Christians are still meeting together on a regular basis; they sing worships songs, take up offerings, listen to sermons, and engage in typical, congenial banter at the conclusion of morning worship services. But sadly, that's pretty much the extent of their 'Christian' walk.

The definition of the word "unmoved" is as follows:

> **"To remain unaffected by circumstance, emotion, excitement, or passion; to be indifferent, impassive, cold, untouched, unimpressed, unconcerned, unresponsive, unfeeling, dry-eyed, unstirred."**

As I read this definition, I am grief stricken; not only because I know this is true for the typical Christian in America, but also because it far too often describes the condition of my very own heart.

I'm sure that each of us desires to be able to genuinely claim that we live each day of our lives in a full-bore, sold-out, passionate pursuit of Christ and His cause, but if we were to be brutally honest with ourselves, the words that more accurately describe us would be unmoved and numb.

Somehow the years of attending or even serving in church have left us passionless, cold and desensitized to the immutable truths of the Gospel of Jesus Christ. The preaching of the Word simply doesn't seem to move us the way it used to. The songs we sing seem dull and our worship has grown self-centric. Our image of the church has lost its luster and our attitudes and actions have become little more than empty, vain repetitions that we robotically carry out week after week. We've allowed ourselves to become listless and numb, and the tragic truth is that most of us are blissfully unaware of it.

Unmoved and numb—these are condemning words that I realize sound harsh when used in describing the church. But friend, if you're brave enough to take a step back and honestly survey the current state of today's church, I believe you'll agree that these words paint an all-too-accurate portrait of her desperate condition.

While this journey will admittedly be very uncomfortable, I promise that once you embark upon it, your heart and life will be forever transformed in an extraordinary way.

Until we fully understand the dire urgency of our present condition, however, it is impossible to set into motion the changes necessary to alter the spiritual course of not only our generation, but that of future generations as well.

While I've met very few Christians in my life who would admit to being spiritually deficient, their lives betray the real truth of the matter. For the sake of argument, let us suppose for a moment that the vast majority of the church isn't spiritually numb. What other reason could we possibly give as to why so many Christians are content to sit in silence as an entire generation slips into hell, our freedoms are stripped away, pre-born babies are murdered in their mothers' womb, lies are exalted, truth is called hate, our children are brainwashed, morality is ridiculed, and we've adopted the view that sharing the Gospel of Jesus Christ is little more than an exercise in futility.

The reason, simple yet disturbing, that we do not stand together against these atrocities is because we've become lulled into complacency and have been rendered nearly incapable of feeling.

We've become spiritually anesthetized by the tolerance and, dare I say, glamorization of sin within our culture. Although we know that biblically these things are wrong, unfortunately they just don't bother us anymore. We are no longer pricked at the heart over the things that grieve God, and our indifference to sin results in little or no motivation for us to even acknowledge or address it.

As Christians, we've allowed ourselves to become comfortable with the way things are, because if we weren't we would feel morally obligated to do something about them. Whenever we experience pain, it is our nature to instinctively respond. When we see someone in danger, we don't just sit back and simply hope everything turns out alright, but that is precisely the attitude that we in America have embraced today. We tend to think that somebody else will do it or that it's up to the pastors, leaders, and teachers to make a difference in the world. Our actions, or rather the lack thereof, clearly demonstrate a disturbing absence of genuine compassion for the perishing.

So what is it that causes us to shift from being on fire for God every day of the week to becoming nothing more than an occasional Sunday morning pew-warmer? Well, for most, it is a very gradual process. As our excitement begins to fade at the hearing of the preaching of the Word of God, our prayer lives diminish nearly to the point of non-existence. Our Bible study falls victim to our hectic schedules, and our soul soon loses its hunger for these life-enriching truths.

Our once vibrant walk with God devolves into an oppressive list of do's and don'ts, and we eventually adopt a 'been there, done that' attitude toward church and we see very little reason to continue attending.

The bottom line is this: The church in America has become listless and irrelevant because it seems preferable to remain comfortably numb than it is to live out our faith spurred on by the same compassion and heartbreak for the lost exemplified by our Savior.

It is only when you and I come to realize that if nothing changes and we continue on day after day down the path we're on, that it will only be a matter of time until the once mighty church in America that has long stood as the beacon of the Gospel's light to the world, fades into nothing more than a fond memory. But the decision to do something about this mustn't wait, and it doesn't start with the pastor in the pulpit or the church member sitting in the pew next to you on Sunday morning. It starts with you and me. Right here—right now.

# CHAPTER 2

## Desperate Times Call For ...Complacent Christians?

> *"Complacency is a deadly foe of all spiritual growth. Acute desire must be present or there will be no manifestation of Christ to His people. He waits to be wanted. Too bad that with many of us He waits so long, so very long, in vain." – A.W. Tozer*

It is my sincere belief that the situation in America is desperate, but unfortunately the church lacks this sense of urgency. Christianity is becoming more and more demonized in secular culture, the name of our Lord is constantly being dishonored and blasphemed by society, and the truths that our forefathers died to preserve are being abandoned as obsolete 'hate speech'. Let there be no doubt about it: Our godly heritage is under attack and is rapidly crumbling, and for all practical purposes it would seem that the average church in America couldn't care less.

As I witness the events in America unfolding today, I find myself asking what it will take to rouse Christians from their slumber. Sadly, though, it would seem that most Christians are content to leave things the way they are. We don't want to rock the proverbial boat, and we certainly wouldn't want to make waves for anybody else. It seems to be the single remaining goal of many churches to hold on to the sliver of relevance they still possess while having no apparent vision of gaining ground and advancing the cause of Christ.

We like to claim that we serve a God who's as mighty today as He was in Bible times, that the blood of Jesus is still the only cure for the sin-sick soul, and that the Word of God is as powerful today as it's ever been. But all too often our lifestyles indicate that we serve a weak, anemic God whom we worship when we feel like it, we have a faith that isn't worth sharing with those around us, and we cling to a gospel that we view as archaic and irrelevant, and then we wonder why the world wants nothing to do with our Jesus. When those outside the faith judge the relevancy of Christianity based upon what they hear us say or what they see us do, the latter will prevail every time. As Ralph Waldo Emerson once said, "Your actions speak so loudly, I cannot hear what you are saying."

You're probably thinking, "I understand the way things are in America and the world. I'm not stupid. I watch the news, I see what's going on, and I'm not happy about it." Great! I'm glad you're not. I hope that it bothers you as much as it bothers me when we see the spiritual war that's being waged all around us today; a war that often times seems so one-sided.

While we're not talking about being 'happy' with the status quo of the average church today, what we are talking about is *complacent Christians.* The word 'complacent' is defined as, "To be pleased with oneself or one's merits, advantages, situation, etc., *often without awareness of some potential danger or defect*; <u>self-satisfied</u>."

You won't have to look far to find someone willing to tell you that they are unhappy with the church today, but what is rare is finding someone who would be honest enough to admit that they need to be doing more to actively engage in the spiritual warfare which permeates our earthly realm.

If I were to ask you to name five people in your life who are completely disengaged, spiritually speaking, it probably wouldn't take you long to create that list. So go ahead and give it a try. It's easy for us to identify other people who we deem lacking in their Christian walk, but it can be far more difficult to objectively assess the condition of our own hearts.

We must begin our personal assessment by asking ourselves a few questions: Is my walk with God a top priority in my life? Have I grown complacent in my attitudes and my actions toward the things of God? Am I so consumed by the worries and stresses of life that I neglect to serve my Lord in the way that I know I should?

There are very few things as damaging to the cause of Christ as a complacent Christian. The time to mobilize the body of Christ for spiritual battle is today. The time to do something is now! For years we've sat idly by and watched the world, the flesh, and the devil strip us of our God-given power, purpose, and passion. We've exchanged purpose for passivity, passion for pleasure, perseverance for preference, principle for peace, truth for tolerance, and ultimately victory for defeat.

The stark reality of the matter, and one which breaks my heart, is the fact that no one, not even the devil himself, could have done this to us. We've done it to ourselves. God's Word declares in Matthew 16:18b "...upon this rock I will build my church; and the gates of hell shall not prevail against it." If even the very gates of hell are scripturally predestined to fail, then the reason we are failing is clear; we have no one to blame but ourselves. There is no one else for us to point our fingers at. Each of us as Christians is guilty. It wasn't just the pastors, the teachers, the politicians, or the evangelists who permitted the moral decay to devastate our land. The sooner we accept the fact that it's entirely up to us to impact this world and be used of God to turn the tides of evil, the closer we will be to experiencing true revival.

One thing potentially even more damaging to Christianity than complacency is believers who refuse to open their eyes and hearts and remain unwilling to take immediate and necessary action to discard their complacency before it destroys not only themselves, but the godly heritage that belongs to future generations. What America and the world needs now is Christians who are on fire for the Lord and are eager and prepared to do whatever it takes to boldly reach the lost with the Gospel of Christ.

# CHAPTER 3

## The High Cost of "Comfortable" Christianity

*"This hill, though high, I covet to ascend; the difficulty will not me offend. For I perceive the way to life lies here. Come, pluck up, heart; let's neither faint nor fear. Better, though difficult, the right way to go, than wrong, though easy, where the end is woe."* *- John Bunyan*

We live in a world that is inundated with technology and conveniences that promise to make our lives more comfortable—more enjoyable. We live in a country with an abundance of drive-thru fast food joints, 24-hour convenience stores, and ever evolving technologies that promise a better 'user experience'. Our society has grown lazy and has developed an unhealthy fixation on wanting to do things the easy way, and you will have to admit that almost every aspect of our lives has been re-engineered with comfort in mind.

Despite all of the blessings that we still enjoy, the relative health and wealth of American society has done more to harm our attitudes and mindsets than practically anything else. We, as a nation, are exceedingly wealthy and blessed, whether we realize it or not. To put this into perspective, someone living at the poverty level in the United States is still in the top 14% of the global income distribution. In fact, there are more than a billion people in the world living on less than $1 per day. Most of us could never begin to imagine living without the modern comforts that we've become accustomed to, such as electricity, running water, an abundance of food, nice cars, heating and cooling, microwave ovens—the list goes on and on.

Now before you jump to the conclusion that I despise all things convenient and comfortable and that I eschew technology, please allow me to explain. I do not believe that there is anything inherently wrong with the comforts that we've come to know and love, in and of themselves, but I do know the dangers that accompany our 'entitlement' attitude. When we forget that the conveniences that we enjoy are luxuries and not privileges, we are setting ourselves up for failure.

We must understand that these comforts come at a high price, even for those of us living here in America. An increasing percentage of our budgets these days is dedicated to ensuring our continued comforts and conveniences. We've all felt the financial pinch at the gas pump while filling our tanks, yet we pay it. We groan at the grocery checkout at the ever rising cost of our favorite foods, but we still buy them. We complain about the exorbitant cost of heating and cooling our homes, but we resentfully write the check each month to ensure that we're sitting in 68° comfort.

The point is that we've become accustomed to paying a high price for comfort, and we're fine with that. This is because the cost didn't overtake us overnight, but rather has crept upon us slowly, generation after generation, until we now pay for these 'necessities' without ever giving it a second thought. We can no longer imagine life without these luxuries, and it seems that we are willing to pay any price to preserve these conveniences we've come to love.

Now, let's apply these same principles and truths to the spiritual realm. In America, we've taken the same approach to Christianity that we've taken to life in general; our religious expectations and desires have also become focused on convenience and comfort. The current trend sweeping through our churches is a wholesale rebranding and promoting of a 'better user experience' as the primary selling feature. The focus of the church has undergone a paradigm shift from scriptural significance to cultural capitulation.

When people are seeking a church to attend, they usually begin by asking themselves questions such as these: What can the church do for me? Do they play the types of music that I enjoy? Are the services short enough so they won't consume too much of my time? Are they going to relentlessly beg me for money? Is the Pastor going to get all 'preachy' and take this church thing way too seriously?

Unfortunately, the vast majority of individuals today aren't looking for anything more than a comfortable place to come, grab a latte, sit for an hour, and hope God notes their dutiful attendance and pastes a shiny gold star beside their name in His holy attendance book.

In much the same way that we're demanding more and more from the technology that we use each day, the 'wow' factor that we've come to expect from the church has grown proportionately. We believe that it's the church's job to constantly come up with new ways to captivate us and enhance our user experience. We want the big buildings, bright lights, loud music, soft chairs, short and sweet sermons, tear jerking analogies, and all the life enhancements that the we feel we're entitled to.

While there's not necessarily anything wrong with many of these things, in and of themselves, this attitude of entitlement to comfort and convenience has sent the average church scrambling to find new ways of meeting these increasing demands, even at the cost of sacrificing the purpose, power, blessing, and anointing of God. They feel that their only option to fill the pews is to submit to the whims of the masses; adopting the world's newest mega-marketing fads to make the service more attractive and inviting for their 'consumers.' This results in an emotional, entertaining experience that tragically produces superficial Christians who have little impact on the direction of this country, the world, or the Kingdom of God.

The sobering truth, however, is that we aren't the only ones paying the price. The eternal burden of our apathy is also being borne by the dying lost who have never heard the gospel. It's further funded by an entire generation who has never seen the mighty hand of God sweep this nation in revival. Meanwhile, we sit in the comfort of our church sanctuary and write checks to pay the bills whilst neglecting all that our forefathers in the faith held precious and dear.

We must remember that God never promised that the Christian life would be easy. There will be hardships and battles—often daily. This has been true for every Christian since the time of Christ, so why should we be any different? Don't become discouraged when things get a little rough; remember you're not alone. God promises us that He will see us through the trials and storms that we face, so let's press onward for Him.

We are called to be soldiers of Christ, not complacent churchgoers. There is an old song written by Isaac Watts entitled, "Am I a Soldier of the Cross?" that I feel says this so well:

> **'Am I a soldier of the cross, a follower of the Lamb, and shall I fear to own His cause or blush to speak His Name?**
>
> **Must I be carried to the skies on flow'ry beds of ease, while others fought to win the prize, and sailed through bloody seas?**
>
> **Are there no foes for me to face? Must I not stem the flood? Is this vile world a friend to grace, to help me on to God?**
>
> **Sure I must fight if I would reign; Increase my courage, Lord. I'll bear the toil, endure the pain, supported by Thy Word.'**

It's time that you and I took an accounting of our hearts and asked ourselves a couple of sobering questions. Have we allowed our entitlement attitude to constrict the way that we live for our Savior, and are we so vain as to imagine that there will be no hardships to face as we share our faith with the world? God forbid.

# CHAPTER 4

## The Rise of the Spiritual Politician

*"...For they loved the praise of men more than the praise of God." – John 12:43*

There is no denying that we live in a politically correct society as our culture is under enormous pressure to compromise and adopt the ways of the world. We're constantly being coerced into changing the way we talk, the places we go, and even our foundational morals and principles, all to ensure that the truth doesn't offend those who don't want to hear it. The paralyzing fear that has resulted seems to have gripped the vast majority of our nation, including our churches.

The tsunami of moral relativism crashing over our land has given rise to a new breed of Christian that I refer to as the 'spiritual politician.' The spiritual politician voluntarily resigns his effectiveness in advancing the cause of Christ by opting for the safety of silence over the peril of speaking the truth. Rather than taking a bold stand, they are quick to compromise. They esteem worldly popularity over the adulation of God, and they would rather bask in the praises of man than pay the significant cost required to effectively impact the world for Christ.

So why does this phenomenon exist? I believe there are several things that give rise to the spiritual politician, and the first is the immense pressure to conform to the world's mold of what a Christian should look like. While certainly not everyone is a Christian, *everyone* seems to have an opinion of what a 'good Christian' is supposed to be, and they have absolutely no problem whatsoever letting you know when you've stepped outside of the 'Christian' box they've created for you. Invariably, when we fall short of their 'standard of excellence', we face the onslaught of ridicule, insults, and outright persecution that they feel we deserve.

The dictionary defines a politician as, "a seeker or holder of public office, who is more concerned about winning favor or retaining power than about maintaining principles." The spiritual politician believes that if he or she is ever going to possess relevance in the eyes of the world, they must first win the world's favor. The motivation of these well-intentioned spiritual politicians is to wield their influence to sway the world for Christ, and this is commendable. The problem, however, is that the results rarely, if ever, match the intention. Compromising in order to gain favor usually results in charges of hypocrisy, and rightfully so. In fact, mainstream society has labeled the church a crutch for the weak-minded hypocrite.

We must understand, however, that merely winning the world's favor is no guarantee that we have achieved any measure of spiritual influence with them. The spiritual politician often makes the fatal error of equating favor and popularity with relevance and impact. Our motivation must derive solely from a heartfelt desire to share the gospel with the lost and see them equipped, motivated, and activated into the service of the Lord. If our purpose is to build the kingdom by impacting our sphere of influence with the Word and power of God, then that's precisely what we should be doing.

The problem arises in thinking that in order to effectively reach the world, we need to fit in with them, walk the way they walk, talk the way they talk, embrace the values they embrace, and above all, avoid offending or daring to contradict them in any way. Newsflash! You will never beget change without confrontation. If we are going to effect change in this country, then we must be willing to compassionately confront it with the unyielding truths of the Word of

God.

Truth, by its very nature, is confrontational. It establishes the boundaries between right and wrong and exposes everything else as lies. It turns the grays into black and white and leaves no room for doubt while impacting the human heart in a way that nothing else can. There is nothing in this world that can break the hardened heart, warm the icy soul, or burn as a fire like the truth of God's Word.

> **"Is not my word like as a fire? saith the Lord; and like a hammer that breaketh the rock in pieces?" – Jeremiah 23:29**

The spiritual politician can be found throughout the church, but more often than not they can be found standing in the pulpit. When any God-ordained preacher or teacher of the Word compromises truth to appease men rather than honor and obey God, it would be far better for him if he vacated the pulpit and let someone else stand and deliver the Word.

I realize the boldness and even the harshness of this statement, but the man of God has never been called to be popular or even loved. His call, rather, is to stand and proclaim without fear the pure, unadulterated Word of the living God. The man of God must be bold without being belligerent, and loving, yet unyielding while passionately burning for his Savior as he imparts the Word.

> **"Preach the word; be instant in season, out of season; reprove, rebuke, exhort with all long suffering and doctrine. For the time will come when they will not endure sound doctrine; but after their own lusts shall they heap to themselves teachers, having itching ears; And they shall turn away their ears from the truth, and shall be turned unto fables. But watch thou in all things, endure afflictions, do the work of an evangelist, make full proof of thy ministry."** -2 Timothy 4:2-5

We must bear in mind, however, that the pulpit isn't the only place that has been co-opted by the spiritual politician; he is found in the pew as well. The responsibility to proclaim the truth of God's Word doesn't rest entirely upon the pulpit. Each of us has been commanded to share the Gospel of Jesus Christ with everyone we come into contact with. This directive is often referred to as the Great Commission. (Matthew 28:18-20) Our attempt to shirk our obligation to witness and to cast it upon those in "full-time Christian service" is nothing short of shameful. If we are waiting for the pastors, teachers, and evangelists to single-handedly turn the tide of evil in this nation, our slide toward destruction will continue unabated. They cannot do it alone, nor should they be expected to.

It is the calling of every Christ-follower to win souls, to pray, to read and study the Word of God, to edify the brethren, and to encourage and enable our leaders to do the same. Each of us is able—no, expected—to reach Heaven from our knees and lead sanctified lives which honor the Lord.

What America needs today is an army of dedicated men and women who love their Lord and have a compassion for the lost that compels them to take a stand and boldly speak the truth in love. It is only then that we can expect to experience the power and moving of the Holy Spirit and bring about the Heaven sent revival that this land so desperately cries out for.

# CHAPTER 5

## Sleeping in the Sanctuary

*"Today Lucifer is probably surveying the church just as Bonaparte did China. One can almost behold the fear in his eyes as he thinks of the Church's unmeasured potential and growls, "Let the Church sleep! If she wakes, she will shake the world." Is not the Church the sleeping giant of today?" – Leonard Ravenhill*

By now I trust that you are fully aware that we are indeed in a war. Not a physical war, mind you, but rather a spiritual one. Our enemy is the flesh, sin, and Satan, and our Commander-in-Chief is the Lord Jesus Christ. Our weapon is the Word of God, and our strength and power to endure this battle comes from God alone. The unacceptable casualties of this war are the innumerable lost heading for eternal damnation every minute of every hour of every day. Time is of the essence, and the time to fight is now.

Not only is the enemy destroying the souls of the lost, he is also relentlessly attacking the faith and effectiveness of Christians as well. He's cold, calculating, powerful, and determined. On our own, we don't stand a chance against him.

Thank God we're not alone! Our Savior has won the battle for us on the cross of Calvary! Our salvation has been secured, and all the power we need to prevail is at our disposal. If we lose this battle in reaching the world for Christ, we have no one to blame but ourselves. For it is Christ Himself who fights alongside us, and as the Apostle Paul said, "If God be for us, who can be against us?" – Romans 8:31b. We Christians aren't simply fighting *for* the victory, we're fighting *from* the victory that we've already secured in Christ!

The problem is that much of the church in America today is either unaware of the war that rages on, or they are simply distracted and indifferent. Regardless, many of the Christians occupying the pews of the church today are unprepared for battle. Our enemy, on the other hand, has been skillfully orchestrating and successfully executing his plan for millennia and has been extremely effective, not because we are powerless to stop it, but because we have been busy pursuing every trinket and bauble the world has to offer.

Winston Churchill, the Prime Minister of England during the Second World War and widely regarded as one of the greatest wartime leaders of the $20^{th}$ century, said of England prior to Nazi Germany's expansion,

"While England slept, Germany prepared for war." He was referring to the fact that England was lying dormant while an unseen war was on the verge of breaking out, and they nearly waited too long to respond to the threat. It was the wake-up call that England and the rest of the world received, combined with the resulting actions they took to organize and mount a resistance, which enabled them to emerge victorious in the war.

I fear the same thing can be said of the church today. For years now, we have been blissfully going about our daily business as if nothing spiritual was going on behind the scenes. Meanwhile, the devil has been strategically stripping Christians of their God-given power, righteousness, influence in society, and the will to engage this battle.

The church has been fast asleep, cradled in their stained-glass fortresses rather than preparing for war. As a result, God has been kicked out of our public school system, the lies of evolution and atheism have corrupted our young people, our culture is actively promoting the 'virtues' of sexual deviancy and promiscuity, thousands of pre-born babies are being 'legally' slaughtered daily, all while the church in America is busy simply trying to cling to the tiny parcel of moral ground that it still possesses. I fear that if the church does not immediately hearken to the wake-up call resounding throughout this land, we will miss what very well may be our last chance to experience revival in America.

If we honestly believe that continuing to do the same things that we've always done and expecting lasting spiritual change or revival to result, then we are willingly ignorant and blind. It's high time that believers realize that the Christian life is about a whole lot more than simply showing up to church once a week. Actually, there is not one shred of scripture that supports the practice of believers living half-hearted Christian lives. Christ didn't die to merely purchase a fragment of our lives; all that we have we owe to Him. If we think we've fulfilled our Christian obligation by dedicating to Him one hour of our time each week, then we surely deserve to watch this nation fade into the pages of history.

At the end of the day when the church lights go out, the stage is dark, and the pews are empty, the spiritual battle relentlessly marches on. If the church continues to sleep while the enemy advances, then we've chosen to give Satan something that he could never have taken from us; our power, purpose, and our passion for Christ. If you and I are content to wait for someone else to wake up to these truths and initiate revival, then the lost will continue to suffer the eternal consequences of our apathy. For the love of God, we ***must not*** allow this to happen any longer!

# CHAPTER 6

## The Trampled Truth

*"The truth is incontrovertible. Malice may attack it, ignorance may deride it, but in the end, there it is."*
*– Winston Churchill*

If there is one thing that has been ruthlessly trampled underfoot by our society and dragged through the mud by our culture, it is truth. Many people hate the truth and work desperately to destroy it, but there is something wonderful about truth, and that is it *always* stands. You may choose to ignore it, yet truth remains. You can try to drown out the voice of truth with the lies of the world, but the truth will still be heard.

The eternal truth of God's Word is our final authority; it always has been, and it always will be. The truth is always relevant and it will never lose its power. God's Word brings clarity to confusion, light to darkness, power to the weak, and restores order where there is chaos. It is the element that is missing from so many areas of society and culture, and a revolution of truth is the only thing that can restore the church and the nation.

Truth is the answer, plain and simple. It almost seems overly simplistic; but in reality, the truth of God's Word has always been the cure for the sin-sick soul, the biting sting of the devil's lies, and the blinding darkness of this world. It has always troubled me that as Christians we always seem to compromise by looking to the methods and solutions of the world for the answers to the problems we face. The Word of God alone is powerful enough to revolutionize not only *our* lives, but the lives of anyone willing to embrace it.

While it may seem very basic, one of the first truths that we must learn is the fact that absolute truth actually exists. Our society has attempted to re-define truth as nothing more than scientific facts. They claim that truth is whatever you wish it to be and it is a matter of personal interpretation; there is no absolute right and wrong. The term for this view is "moral relativism." Moral relativism is the view that moral judgments are true or false only relative to some particular standpoint (for instance, that of a culture or a historical period) and that no standpoint is uniquely privileged over all others. The reality of the matter, however, is there *are* absolutes in this life; there *are* eternal truths that are undeniable, irrefutable, and are found only in the Word of God—the source of *all* truth.

The next inherent truth that the world must hear is that there is one true God and lawgiver who is alive and well and seated on the throne of Heaven. The lie that men and women have somehow been granted the ability to re-define what sin is and what it is not has deceived millions into believing that there will be no consequences for the lifestyles that they choose to live.

The truth is that God doesn't give us a list of dos and don'ts to deprive, control, or inconvenience us, but rather to protect us and provide benefit and blessing.

Much to the dismay of many, the truth doesn't change simply because we choose to ignore it, nor does it go away because we remain willfully ignorant of it. Statistically speaking, there are over 150,000 people passing through death's door each and every day. These souls will be spending eternity somewhere, and you and I possess the power and the obligation to help them make an informed decision regarding their ultimate destination.

Unbelievers have long portrayed God as some cranky, white-haired old man sitting up in heaven with a lightning bolt in one hand and pointing His finger at them with the other just waiting for them to step out of line so He can zap them. But the God of heaven is gracious and loving and cares so much about us that even in our sinful state He reached out to us in sacrificial love.

> **"But God commendeth his love toward us, in that, while we were yet sinners, Christ died for us." - Romans 5:8**

Although the truth is scorned by society, rejected by the God-haters, ignored by the arrogant, and unknown to the ignorant; truth still endures! In the public eye the divine truth might never be viewed as an asset or a priority, but that will never diminish its power to set the captive free, give sight to the blind, and salvation to the lost soul. Yes, the everlasting truth of the Word of God is our only weapon in this spiritual war, and it is up to us to wield that weapon with skill and determination.

There is something inside each of us as humans that inherently desires to know the truth. It's a gnawing curiosity; a hunger that can only be satisfied by the Word of God. People today, just as they have for thousands of years, are still searching in all the wrong places for the peace that can only be obtained through a relationship with Jesus Christ. Pontius Pilate, the politician that sentenced Jesus to be crucified, was driven to ask Jesus the burning question that he so deeply needed answered, "What is truth?"

> **"Pilate therefore said unto him, Art thou a king then? Jesus answered, Thou sayest that I am a king. To this end was I born, and for this cause came I into the world, that I should bear witness unto the truth. Every one that is of the truth heareth my voice. Pilate saith unto him, What is truth? And when he had said this, he went out again unto the Jews, and saith unto them, I find in him no fault at all."** - John 18:37-38

We find Jesus' answer from the Savior's own mouth in John 17:17 when He said, speaking to His Heavenly Father, "Thy Word is truth."

What the world needs from the church today isn't a performance. They don't need us to put on a show or 'wow' them with the talents and gifts that God has given us. They aren't looking for the 'next big thing' and they don't need entertained. Whether they know it or not what the world needs is the pure, wholesome truth found in the pages of God's Word. They need to hear us speaking and living what we say we believe, not only on Sunday but every day of the week; in the workplace, the gas station, the grocery store, the schoolhouse, and the public square. The era of the hallelujah hypocrite must end.

# CHAPTER 7

## Called to Care—Genuine or Imitation?

*"If sinners be damned, at least let them leap to Hell over our dead bodies. And if they perish, let them perish with our arms wrapped about their knees, imploring them to stay. If Hell must be filled, let it be filled in the teeth of our exertions, and let not one go unwarned and unprayed for." – Charles H. Spurgeon*

Today, more than perhaps any other time in the history of this nation, we are suffering from a lack of authenticity. We live in a day and age where everything seems to be a facade with people hiding behind the ornately painted theatrical masks they want others to see. Unfortunately, we Christians also feel the need to hide who we really are. We're afraid of how others might perceive us if they knew of our vulnerabilities, weaknesses, and shortcomings.

The thought seems to be that if we are anything short of the professional, well-rounded, flawless, Christ-like individuals people expect us to be, then we are doomed to be failures both in our secular lives as well as within the church, when in fact nothing could be further from the truth. What the world so desperately seeks these days is a meaningful relationship with genuine, transparent people who choose not to conceal their humanness, and it can easily spot a fake from a mile away. Authenticity is an invaluable asset that will enable you to relate to and connect with those who may be struggling in their lives.

Basically, people want to know that you genuinely care. As the old saying goes, "people don't care how much you know until they know how much you care." This is fundamentally true regardless of your background, culture, or personality. There are precious few things that will more readily compel people to drop the walls that separate them from the message of Christ than believing that you genuinely care for them.

This truth became real to me years ago during a revival meeting that was being held at the Belmont Correctional Institution in southern Ohio while I was working with Rock of Ages prison ministry. At the end of the first night's service, I was standing with several other preachers in the back of the Chapel saying goodbye to the men and encouraging them to come back the next night. As one man was leaving, I asked him if he planned on retuning for the next evening's service. He paused and said, "You know, I've heard a lot better preaching in my time, but yes, I will be back tomorrow night." I asked him why he was planning on coming back, and he replied, "Two reasons. First, you guys seem real. We may be in prison, but we can spot a fake a mile away. Second, because you guys love us, and that's something that we hardly ever see."

Caring and compassion are what's missing from much of society today. Why don't we see more Christians sharing the gospel and why aren't we standing up for truth and against the lies of the enemy? Because we don't care enough to sacrifice our comfort by preserving and living out the heritage passed down to us in the Word of God.

The issue isn't that we fail to say that we care, because our *words* would have the world believe that their lives and eternity sincerely do matter to us. But the problem is that casually verbalizing our care isn't enough; talk is cheap. We are called not only to care, but to also demonstrate compassion which is made up of two concepts, the first being that we are conscious of the condition of those around us. We can never forget that hell is burning just as hot right now as it was 2,000 years ago and that people who die without Christ today still face those same eternal flames. When we forget the hopeless condition of this world apart from our Lord, it's only a matter of time before the only thing demonstrated by our actions and attitudes is an apathetic counterfeit of true Christianity.

The second component of compassion consists of a strong desire to eradicate the pain and danger that we know others needlessly face. In other words, compassion should compel us to do all that we can to reach out to those who don't know Jesus. Christ didn't merely say that He cared for the lost world, He left no doubt about it when He stepped into the world as a baby, lived a sinless life, and willingly sacrificed Himself on the cross of Calvary to pay for the sins of the world. Compassion was the compelling force behind every action He took. It wasn't acceptance, popularity, fame, or money; all He wanted was to reach those who so badly needed Him, and this too should be the motivation that fuels our own lives and ministries.

Without compassion our faith is useless to the world because it is devoid of love, concern, and urgency. It is impossible to overstate the power and impact of truly caring for others. When we interact with the world in a genuine, convincing, and compassionate manner, the walls of division crumble and hearts become pliable and receptive to the life-saving message of the gospel.

# CHAPTER 8

## The Power of Passion

*"The most powerful weapon on earth is the human soul on fire." – Ferdinand Foch*

Regardless of your background, education, philosophy, or faith, we are all creatures of passion. It speaks to us and guides us in the decisions that we make and the paths that we choose in life. Yes, passion rules us all. In fact, we live our entire lives in a contentious state suspended between the pursuit and denial of these passions. Everything that we have ever achieved in life can be attributed to the influence and manifestation of passion. Without passion we would be but hollow, cold, listless creatures. Without passion, we would not live, but merely exist.

There is no force in this world more powerful than passion. It drives people to places they never dreamed they could go and makes them behave in ways they never thought they were capable of; driving them to actions that would otherwise be utterly unthinkable.

We're all familiar with the scripture that says that the love of money is the root of all evil, but if we zoom out and look at the big picture we discover that it is ultimately passion that is responsible for every action we take, both good and evil. Upon examination, it's apparent that every crime, every war, every divorce, every lie, and even every angry word that's ever been spoken can be traced back to man's primeval passions. Conversely, every good thing that has ever come into existence was also birthed from passion. Books are written, pictures are painted, songs are composed, mountains are climbed, careers are pursued, relationships are formed, and children and dreams are all conceived of passion.

The problem remains that we are born with a broad range of passions including those that are inherently sinful. Consequently, these natural inclinations that we possess at birth invariably lead us into direct conflict with our Creator.

Ultimately what we lack is a deep, abiding, fiery passion for the things of God. If you are expecting to miraculously awaken one day with a burning passion for Christ, you're likely in for a very long wait. While passions are part of our natural being, they can change over time. The sinful passions come naturally to us, but the spiritual, godly passions are instilled in us when we trust Jesus as our Lord and Savior. When we commit our lives to Christ, our desires and attitudes are changed. In much the same way that we attempt to align ourselves with the desires, likes, and dislikes of our spouse over the years, we also embrace and adopt the passions of Christ the longer we serve Him.

The purpose of the Christian life is to pursue an intimate relationship with Christ. It sounds pretty simple, and that's because it is. As with so many things in life, it ain't rocket surgery. When you passionately pursue Christ every day of your life, then everything else will fall into place because the closer you get to the Lord, the more His priorities become your priorities, His passions your passions, His dislikes your dislikes, His attitude your attitude, and ultimately His heart your heart. If there was but one thing that I could encourage you to do in life, it would be to passionately and relentlessly pursue God every single day.

You don't have to tell a sold-out follower of Christ to pray and read their Bible every day because they're already doing it. They have an insatiable desire to spend time with God and get to know Him on a deeper level. One who is pursuing the Lord doesn't have to be told to avoid sin because it is their desire to please their loved one. The Christian who walks daily with Jesus doesn't have to be forced to share their faith with others because they are so excited about it that their passion consumes every aspect of their life and others can't help but notice the evidence of their relationship with God.

The longer you walk with the Lord the more closely your heart beats in sync with His, and the world around you dims in comparison to Him.

> **"But what things were gain to me, those I counted loss for Christ. Yea doubtless, and I count all things but loss for the excellency of the knowledge of Christ Jesus my Lord: for whom I have suffered the loss of all things, and do count them but dung, that I may win Christ, and be found in him, not having mine own righteousness, which is of the law, but that which is through the faith of Christ, the righteousness which is of God by faith:**
>
> **That I may know him, and the power of his resurrection, and the fellowship of his sufferings, being made conformable unto his death;" - Philippians 3:7-10**

Helen Lemmel, like the Apostle Paul, also found this to be true and penned these words to the hymn *"Turn Your Eyes Upon Jesus"*

**"Turn your eyes upon Jesus,**
**Look full in His wonderful face,**
**And the things of earth will grow strangely dim,**
**In the light of His glory and grace."**

There is nothing in this entire world that compares to walking with Jesus; it's an unquenchable fire that burns continually within my heart. Each day, in spite of the trials and tribulations that come my way, my walk with the Lord grows sweeter and sweeter. What an honor and a privilege to think that the Creator of the entire universe desires a deep and daily relationship with each of us. Don't we owe at least that much to the Savior who willingly sacrificed His life on a cross to pay for our sins; a debt that we could never have paid? Shouldn't the temporary pleasures, fleeting moments of happiness, and short-lived success in this world pale in comparison to our walk with Jesus Christ? Yes! Yes! A thousand times yes!

So what's the problem? Why aren't more Christians on fire for the Lord? Sadly, I believe it's because we are more passionate about worldly concerns than we are about the Savior that died to know us. Stop and think about that for a minute. Christ left heaven, sacrificing all of its comfort and convenience, lived a sinless life, and was voluntarily and brutally crucified, yet we bel-lyache about 'giving up' an hour of our week to worship Him? Do we honestly think that we are somehow justified by this meager act of 'sacrifice'? God help us, if we do!

Passion is what drove our Lord to reach out and touch the lost and hurting despite the cruel nails in His hands. He endured the searing pain in His feet inflicted by the iron spikes to travel to those in need. Despite the horrific wounds on His whip shredded back, He continued to carry our cross. Blood flowed from His thorn crowned head, yet didn't stop Him from speaking the truth to those who would listen. His spear pierced side flowed forth blood from his broken heart while He uttered those fateful words, "It is finished!"

The passion that Jesus has for us is what made His sacrifice possible. The salvation that He bought and the relationship that it yielded is what made it profitable. With all that He's done for us, how on earth can we possibly be content with our lack of passion and zeal for Him?

Nothing but a burning heart, fueled by passion, can sustain us through the hard times that lie ahead. There really is no substitute for godly passion, and without it we are just hollow, superficial individuals who are merely play actors vainly playing a role that we call Christianity.

# CHAPTER 9

## From Worrier to Warrior

*"Press forward. Do not stop, do not linger in your journey, but strive for the mark set before you. Fight the good fight of faith, and God will give you spiritual mercies." -George Whitefield*

Considering the condition of our nation and the constant barrage of turmoil tearing away at the world, it's so easy to become overwhelmed with worry. Each day seems to usher in yet another cause for concern; from the Wall Street financial report to the weather report, stress has become an integral component of modern life. Sadly, as the world grows darker and darker the church's increasingly common response has been to withdraw from the culture and concede defeat. Our courage has been replaced with cowardice, our faith with stress, our resolve with retreat, and our boldness with fear. The deterioration of the church combined with our culture's overt hostility toward Christianity seems to have convinced many of us that the battle is lost and our circumstance is hopeless.

But were things really any different in the days of Christ? I don't think so. Most of the issues that cause us concern today have always existed. Wars are certainly nothing new; neither are droughts, economic collapses, tyranny and oppression, nor our propensity to embrace sin. Somehow though we have embraced the notion that the world is worse off now than it's ever been. But if you take an honest look at world history, I believe that it is primarily the church that has deteriorated. While the church once powerfully proclaimed the gospel and stood as the beacon of light and truth in the world, we've now become timid; content to bide our time anxiously wringing our hands as we cower in the shadows of the steeple waiting for the Jesus taxi to whisk us off to glory.

We say that we serve an all-powerful God, but if we truly believe that, why do we spend so much of our lives stressing out over the woes of the world? I say it's because we lack faith, and where there's a lack of faith fear will inevitably flourish. Fear is what keeps us shackled on the sidelines of the spiritual war that's taking place all around us. Oh, that God would raise up men and women who weren't paralyzed by fear and incapacitated by stress and worry! I've heard it said that there are but three types of people in the world: the fearful, the ignorant, and those who read and believe their Bibles.

We have an overabundance of worriers in the church today who are frozen to the pew and are busy enumerating the reasons that revival will never come to America. Enough! God doesn't need worriers—He needs warriors! He needs Christians who are willing to don their spiritual armor and run headlong into the battle; people who are no longer content with warming a church pew on Sunday but are anxious to boldly stand up and take decisive action for the Kingdom of God. The reason that the church is waning and America is relinquishing its Christian heritage is of no fault of the secular world whatsoever. We can't blame the liberals, television, politicians, the Internet, left-wing colleges, public schools, well-funded lobbyists, deceitful philosophies, or even the devil himself for our demise. The blame for these tragedies rests wholly and squarely upon the shoulders of the church.

We have willingly ceased to be the spiritual warriors that God calls us to be. We've come to a place where we openly embrace and tolerate sin rather than opposing it. It's far easier and safer to stay within the confines of the church house than it is to step out and do battle with the enemy, so we choose the paltry existence of a powerless, purposeless, and passionless admirer of baby Jesus rather than a mighty follower of King Jesus. As a result, our impact on the world has been diluted and we shamefully stand in complicit silence as the world rockets toward hell, while faithlessly hoping that our precarious, peaceful, pathetic lifestyles won't be jeopardized by the deceitful wiles of the devil.

I'll say it plainly: we need spiritual warriors who believe and understand that power is exponentially increased when we commit to prayer and fasting. Powerful prayer requires work—it requires sacrifice. Prayer itself is a battle that sadly seems to be a lost art. We pray vague, passionless prayers that present God with an insulting pittance of a sacrifice; one that costs us nothing. As a result, the pathetic excuse we attempt to pass off as a prayer life is rarely little more than periodic, weak, barren, lifeless exercise in futility that is surely a stench in the nostrils of Almighty God. We lack sincerity, urgency and fervency in our prayer lives and then we wonder why our prayers remain unanswered.

> **"The effectual fervent prayer of a righteous man availeth much." - James 5:16b**

There is unspeakable power in prayer, yet rather than fighting in prayer we choose to strive in the flesh. Foolishly we often do battle in our own strength rather than wrestling with the enemy behind the closed door of our prayer closet. We must become prayer warriors who are willing to storm the very gates of hell; tearing down its strongholds and laying waste to its very foundation.

Christ set the example for us when He began His earthly ministry by praying and fasting in the desert for forty days and forty nights. If these elements were so essential that even the Lord of Heaven Himself was steadfastly devoted to them, we are surely missing out on a fundamental necessity of the Christian life when we neglect to make room for them in our 'busy' lives.

As faithful spiritual warriors we have nothing to fear but failing our Lord and succumbing to sin, yet we seem to be petrified by what we perceive as the consequences of unconditionally stepping out and serving our Lord. We fear the opinion of man more than we desire the approval of God. Are there none willing to stand for truth and against sin? If we were to wield but a fraction of the power that we claim to possess, which is our Christian birthright, this world would neither be found in want nor in need of revival today. In Genesis, Esau sold his birthright to Jacob for a bowl of stew. We weren't so shrewd. We squandered ours away and have nary a bean to show for it.

We have been waiting far too long for spiritual warriors to arise who will engage the battle, when we in fact are the ones we've been waiting for. I am fully convinced that if even one tenth of the people occupying the pews of our churches would get engaged in pushing back the veil of darkness and spreading the gospel, worldwide revival would ensue and righteousness would be restored to our land. If we continue to abstain from undertaking the mission that the Lord has called us to, then judgment day will be a sorrowful and regrettable experience for each and every one of us—God forbid it! God, turn us from worriers to warriors before it's too late!

# CHAPTER 10

## Faith in Action

*"We do not segment our lives, giving some time to God, some to our business or schooling, while keeping parts to ourselves. The idea is to live all of our lives in the presence of God, under the authority of God, and for the honor and glory of God. That is what the Christian life is all about." - R.C. Sproul*

Before a contemporary Christian can even consider engaging in aggressive spiritual warfare, we must first cast off any unsound perceptions of what the Christian life actually entails. To be properly and fully equipped, there are several things that we must possess.

First, there must be an awakening and stirring within the heart which can only be accomplished by the Word and the Spirit of Almighty God. Two additional, yet vital elements necessary for sustained revival are vision and passion.

All great plans begin with vision. As Christians we must first have a crystal clear awareness of where we are right now; both as the church as well as a nation. This awareness, while admittedly uncomfortable and unsettling, is absolutely imperative if we are to invoke the changes that need to take place. We must step back and take an objective look at our Christian culture and identify the problems that exist within the church, because as the old adage suggests, "as goes the church, so goes the nation."

Why have we allowed our country to stray so far from our biblical roots? How did we descend into the passionless, powerless, and purposeless moral and spiritual state that we languish in today? Do we believe that God has abandoned us and refuses to endue us with the power on high necessary to stand against the onslaught of the enemy? Do we serve a weak, anemic God? The answer is an emphatic, resounding NO! Make no mistake about it, my friend; had the church not bowed at the altars of materialism and political correctness, had it not watered down the truth, distanced itself from God, shunned the commands of the Bible, and forsaken prayer, we wouldn't be having this discussion and you wouldn't be reading this book.

Since 1 Peter 2:5 tells us that "Ye also, as lively stones, are built up a spiritual house, an holy priesthood, to offer up spiritual sacrifices, acceptable to God by Jesus Christ", the next logical step in establishing our vision is to understand the condition of our own hearts and lives. As painful and difficult as it might be, we have to take a good, long look in the mirror of God's Word to determine if we are where we should be, spiritually speaking. If we harbor sin in our heart, we must repent of it. If anything in this world has become more important to us than our Lord, we must abandon it.

To complete our vision, we must understand the role within the church that God desires each of us to fill. Once we've achieved this, we will experience a glorious revival; a mighty moving of God that will bring about the changes that this world so desperately needs.

The second element that is needed for lasting revival is godly passion. Since we've already spent some time talking about this, I won't tarry long other than to say that when God ignites a passion in your soul that becomes an unquenchable fire, there will undoubtedly be those around you who will warn against becoming 'so heavenly minded that you are of no earthly good.' My friend, if anyone ever says this to you, rest assured that it is highly unlikely that it will ever be said of them. There is no man more valuable to this world than he who walks closely with God. Unleash your passion for God in every aspect of your life; when you do, it will benefit not only you, but the world around you as well.

Christian Evangelist Leonard Ravenhill once said, "A vision without a task makes a visionary; a task without a vision makes drudgery; but a vision with a task makes a missionary." This man of God certainly knew what he was talking about. Without these vital elements present in our hearts and lives, we are doomed to a miserable, impotent Christian existence. It is only when heavenly vision and godly passion collide that we are able to see the fruits of our faith in action. After all, James said under the inspiration of the Holy Spirit, "faith without works is dead." (James 2:26)

The life of the spirit-filled Christian is one of faith, not sight (2 Corinthians 5:7), and we need to become obedient followers who walk and live solely by faith even though we are creatures that prefer to be able to see where we are going. We have a natural aversion to darkness and we prefer not to live in the realm of the unknown, so the idea of living from day to day beyond the limits of our own strength, wisdom, and means tends to scare us to death. To put our faith into action, we must step outside of our comfort zone and relinquish our passive attitudes. The end result will be a dramatic increase in our impact upon this world.

Another component of the Christian faith that the church seems to have compromised is the biblical concept of praise and worship. The writer to the Hebrews says, "By him therefore let us offer the sacrifice of praise to God continually." (Hebrews 13:15) This verse clearly states that our praise to God be continual. This means in the good times as well as in the bad times; when we see the evident moving of God, and also when the heavens seem like brass. We must commit to praising God even when our circumstances may drive us to do the opposite. The fact of the matter is that even when things aren't good, God still is. He is eternally worthy of our worship and praise regardless of the situation we find ourselves in, and this demands a great deal of faith at times.

We also must endeavor to become Christians who are willing to labor by faith. The Apostle Paul penned these words of exhortation to the church, "And let us not be weary in well doing: for in due season we shall reap, if we faint not." (Galatians 6:9) Here we are commanded to continue to labor for the Lord even when we see no evidence that we are accomplishing anything at all. There are few things as discouraging as seemingly fruitless labor. When you pour your heart, time, talents, and resources into the work of the Lord and see little or no return on your investment, the natural thing to do is quit. But as we see here, we have the promise of God that we will see the blessing come *in due season.* In other words, we will see the results in God's time, not necessarily when we want or expect.

Pressing on despite a lack of visible results takes a whole lot of faith.

In the same way that a tool left on the shelf of the workshop accomplishes nothing, our faith when left dormant on the shelf of our life has similar unutilized potential. Although the blight of dead faith has infested America's churches at pandemic levels, we have the cure. That cure is our faith in action.

# CHAPTER 11

## So, What Do I Do Now?

*"Silence in the face of evil is itself evil: God will not hold us guiltless. Not to speak is to speak. Not to act is to act." — Dietrich Bonhoeffer*

It is my most sincere hope that your journey through these pages has left you heartbroken over the condition of the church in America and dissatisfied with the state of your own heart. I also hope that you've come to realize that true revival must begin with you, and that you are now burdened with a deep passion to see revival once again sweep this nation. The questions that logically must follow are, "So now what? Where do I go from here? What are the steps that I need to take to make a difference?" While it's crucial that we understand the situation we're in, it's equally important that we adopt a solid, practical game plan that we can implement in our lives today. I've often said that if it isn't practical, it isn't powerful.

Let's take a moment to examine some of these practical actions. These steps aren't complicated, and frankly they don't need to be. Walking with God isn't nearly as mystic or theological as we often are led to believe or perceive it to be. Keep in mind, however, that just because a spirit-filled and passionate walk with God is not complicated does not mean that it's going to be easy. In fact, to say that a powerful and fulfilling walk with the Lord can be achieved through little effort couldn't be further from the truth. So as we begin to explore the steps that we must take to become effective, productive Christians, bear in mind that these need to be incorporated into your daily life and not merely viewed as temporary actions that you take on those rare occasions when 'the spirit moves you'.

**1. Prayer** - (1 Thessalonians 1:17)

***Live in passionate pursuit of God every day of your life.***

When I say pray, I don't mean just bowing your head to thank God for your meal before you eat. We must embrace the fact that the battle for the souls of men is fought and won in prayer. The devil has no fear at all as you simply sit in your pew on Sunday, but he is absolutely terrified when he sees a prayer warrior hit their knees. Passionate prayer yields more fruit than anything else in the Christian life. Intercessory prayer is work, and hard work at that, but there is no substitute for the power and passion that radiates from a fervent, effectual prayer life. A Christian who isn't praying is playing, so pray hard!

As shocking as this might sound to many Christians, I believe that we should commit to praying for at least one hour a day. Yes, that's right, one hour a day. Is this too much to ask? Didn't Christ give His all for us? If we truly believe that there is power in prayer, then we *must* pray!

What on earth will I pray about for an entire hour though? Well, get yourself a small notebook and start by creating a detailed prayer list as you go throughout your day. You'll be amazed at how many occasions for prayer you can identify in the course of your day-to-day activities. I've never met a great man of prayer that didn't have a great prayer list. Begin your list with an attitude of praise and worship, humbling yourself before God. Acknowledge before the Lord that you are a sinner saved by grace and in desperate need of the mercy and love of Christ. Just as Isaiah did, express your desire to see God high and lifted up! After all, He's the Supreme Creator of the universe and He longs to spend time communing with *you*, so don't take that lightly! Write down all of the reasons that God is worthy of your praise, and friend, you'll find that that's going to be a mighty long list! Praise Him not only for what He's done for you, but also for who He is; your awe-inspiring, loving, Holy Savior.

Next, list the sins in your life. Take the time to confess and forsake each of them before the Lord, leaving nothing out! Repent of your faults and weaknesses to the only one who can forgive and transform you, and you shall be clean.

And finally, take the time to list all of the things that you desperately want to see God do in you, your family, your church, your friends, your community, and your country. List each of them by name, and then commit to pray for each one specifically and individually. Don't go to God with vague requests or meaningless repetitions. Armed with your prayer list, you are now prepared to boldly approach the throne of God and present to Him the list of things that you need Him to do; things that only He can do.

When you pray, do so in faith. Don't profess to serve an almighty and limitless God, and then timidly ask Him for small, insignificant things. You can ask Him for specific things that may seem impossible in the eyes of the world and even to other faith-impaired Christians. Never limit God's power in your prayer closet, for when you do, you hinder His working in your life. When we fail to seek the face of God, how is it that we're surprised when we never see it? When we neglect to plead for the power of God, then it shouldn't shock us when we fail to experience it.

**2. Purpose** - (Matthew 28:18-20)

***You are here for a reason greater than anything your mortal mind can conceive.***

God didn't sacrifice His Son on the cross of Calvary to save our souls just so that you and I could spend our lives aimlessly wandering through life without purpose. God paid an exceedingly high price for the privilege of having fellowship with His creation. He wants to walk with us in the here and now, not just in the sweet by and by. When we fail to grasp the concept that Christ has both a general and a specific purpose for each of us, we are doomed to an empty, powerless, and listless existence as Christians. There is none so miserable in this world as the child of God who fails to live each day of his life within the purpose Christ destined for him.

One would think that it would be relatively easy for us to determine God's purpose for us; however our Christian lives suggest that we are utterly clueless in this regard. It doesn't matter who you are, which spiritual gifts you possess, what your physical circumstances are, or even what sort of personality you have; if you are a born-again child of God, you are called to share the Gospel with the lost. Period. There are no ifs ands or buts about it. That's what Christ said, and that's precisely what He meant.

Consequently, you and I must commit to diligently fulfilling our purpose in sharing the Gospel with the lost every day. Without a doubt, we need to constantly be on the lookout for opportunities to lead someone to Christ. Whether we are sharing God's plan of salvation by handing out a gospel tract, engaging in purposed conversation, or lovingly and passionately confronting somebody with the truth of the Word of God, we must continually ask Him to open doors for us to share the good news, and we can rest assured that He will do just that. We must earnestly pray for opportunities to see the lost saved, and then make the most of these opportunities by the grace and power of God and the leading of His Holy Spirit.

**3. Power** - (2 Corinthians 12:9)

***Never attempt the work of God without the power of God.***

The job of reaching this world with the saving gospel of Jesus Christ is an overwhelming task that can easily discourage us if we are not careful. You might look at the calling on your life and be tempted to say, "There's no way that I can do that!", but the reality is that it is impossible for us to impact the world for the cause of Christ and bring revival to the church in America by our own strength. Our best efforts are doomed to failure if they are made without the blessing and moving of the Holy Spirit.

Admitting that we are weak and unable to achieve what God demands of us outside of His power is the first step in completing these seemingly impossible tasks, but it cannot be overstated that our weakness in no way justifies our apathy. As John the Baptist said, "He must increase, but I must decrease." (John 3:30) The problem is not that the world is seeing too few Christians today, the problem is that they are seeing too much of *us*, and not enough of Christ. If you're operating as a Christian within the limitations of your own comfort and abilities, then you're doing it all wrong!

Ask yourself at the close of each day, "Have the actions that I've taken today, the attitudes I've had, the time that I've spent, and the passions that I've pursued, derived from a power that could only have come from God, or have I chosen to allow my own fleshly desires to dictate my words and actions?" We must constantly strive to live beyond our own power, because it is only then that we are operating in the strength and guidance of the Heavenly Father.

**4. Purity** - (Romans 6:1-2)

***Purity is not measured in the distance between you and sin, but rather in the distance between you and the Savior. The Lord alone is our standard.***

The measure of purity is not found in the distance between you and sin, but rather in the distance between you and the Savior.

Purity is another vital element of the Christian life. We are called to be *in the world* but never *of the world.* There is nothing that will rob the Christian of his power, peace, passion, joy, and impact more than our 'secret' sins. There are no such things as small sins in the eyes of God, and any sins that are harbored in the heart of the believer will ultimately render them practically powerless.

If we intend to reach the lost, we mustn't do it half-heartedly. We cannot live our lives chasing the things of this world, while choosing only to walk with God when it's comfortable or convenient. The Christian life was never intended to be a "part-time job." Everything that we do should flow from our relationship with God.

Sin is to have absolutely no place in the hearts and lives of believers; biblically, there is no question about that. Anyone who attempts to justify their sin before a righteous and holy God is woefully ignorant of the

Scriptures. The point of true purity, however, runs much deeper than the mere absence of sin. While you can refrain from committing many sins, you still may never come close to grasping what the Christian life is really all about. If you doubt the truth of this statement, take a look at the Pharisees of Christ's day. Their lives were consumed with the abstinence of sin, yet they were so far from the God they professed to follow that the only word that could accurately be used to describe them is 'hypocrites.'

As you grow closer and closer to the Lord, you will naturally move away from sin and the things of this world. Purity is the result of our pursuit of Christ, and this inevitably requires the removal of anything that may hinder or slow that pursuit, but the removal of sin should be the by-product of purity, never the goal. As Christ followers, our goal should be to end each day nearer to the Lord than were we at the beginning of it.

We need to ask ourselves, "Has there ever been a time that I was closer to God than I am right now? What is standing in the way of my intimate relationship with Christ? Is there anything that is more important to me than my walk with the Lord?"

**5. Perception** - (Romans 9:1-3)

***To see what Christ sees, we must envision the lost fall-***

***ing into hell.***

If we ever have any hope of remotely understanding, identifying with, and being motivated by the passion that Christ has for lost souls, we must try to grasp the reality of the eternity that awaits the unsaved, and motivation always springs from perception and vision. If we fail to grasp the perception that shaped Christ's actions both while He walked this earth and now as He reigns in heaven, then there is no way that we can ever impact this world as He did.

First, we need to understand that there is no lasting hope for mankind apart from Jesus Christ and His sacrifice on the cross. There is no "12-step program" that can bring peace, healing, and forgiveness to the sin-sick souls of men. Anything but a relationship with Christ serves as little more than a temporary bandage for a very permanent problem. Without the intervention of Christ, mankind is hopelessly lost.

Second, we must come to grips with the stark reality that those who die without accepting the gift of salvation are destined to spend eternity in the lake of fire. But even worse than the relentless flames that burn the souls of the damned, the darkness that engulfs them, or their cries that fall on deaf ears, is their eternal separation from God. There are no human words that can adequately depict this place of sheer torment, but we would each do well solemnly contemplate the cries of the lost from the pit of hell!

The lost man in Luke 16 begged for someone to go to his family to warn them away from the place of his doom that he shares with countless others. My friend, I wonder how our apathy and our relationship with Christ would be impacted if hell were as real to us as it was to that lost man!

**6. Passion** - (Philippians 3:7-10)

***Let your passion for God drive you to live on the brink of eternity every day of your life.***

When God instills His purpose deep within the heart of an individual, there is no cost that they are unwilling to pay to fulfill that passion. The passionate will overcome every obstacle they face, run while others walk, persevere while others quit, and succeed where others fail, and there is nothing that can quench that fire.

Have earthly passions crept into my heart to take the place that belongs to the Lord alone? Have earthly priorities stolen the zeal for the Lord from my heart? Is there anything that I have placed higher than God? If you answered yes to any of these questions, then I would urge you to make things right with God right now, or you will never experience the victory that

Christ provides for us.

**7. Propulsion** - (Hebrews 13:12-14)

***Press past the comfortable so you can achieve the incredible.***

The life of the Disciple of Christ cannot be described as comfortable, and Jesus never said that it would be. If you are looking for comfort, entertainment, and distraction, then you probably need to go see the world and the Devil, because that's their department. But don't you dare come to the house of God professing your desire to become a disciple of Christ and then act surprised when you're smacked upside the head by the world, the flesh, and the Devil. We're in a spiritual war, and I have never heard of a 'comfortable' war, so why do we expect our lives as warriors for Christ to be easy?

There has never been a great accomplishment done for God that did not involve that Christian stepping beyond where they were content, pushing past what was comfortable, and going outside of their personal limitations in order to see God do through them that which would have been impossible by them.

Do I care more about the purpose of Christ than I do about the worldly comfort that I've grown accustomed to? Am I really willing to sacrifice the power, favor, and impact of the Holy Spirit upon the altar of convenience? God deliver us from being content Christians! Woe to them that are at ease in Zion!

**8. Persistence** - (Galatians 6:9-10)

***Never allow your feelings to dictate your actions; continue to push forward in faith.***

I wish I could tell you that once you've employed each of these eight practical principles for Christian living that life will become a bed of roses for you. It would be simply awesome if earnestly doing these things each day of your life would make following Christ comfortable and that you would experience the physical blessings of God beyond your wildest dreams. In reality, however, being a disciple of Christ requires a lot of work, passion, sweat, tears, and yes, sometimes even blood. Living a powerful and effective Christian life requires persistence. It demands our very best day in, day out. It commands us to stay steadfast even in the face of intense ongoing adversity. There's never been a Christian in history that has made an eternal impact on this world that didn't endure a measure of pain and suffering along the way. Persevering through the persecutions that inevitably result from following Christ is simply a part of the Christian experience.

You will find that as you get more and more involved in the battle for the souls of men, the resistance grows stronger and stronger. It will require a level of determination that can only be achieved through the grace and power of Almighty God. Note that the Scripture says that "in due season, we shall reap if we faint not." Unfortunately, God doesn't operate on our timetable. This truth has discouraged many people in the church to the point that they cease serving God altogether. There are few things as discouraging as feeling that your labors for the Lord are in vain.

Becoming a great warrior for Christ is certainly not something that happens overnight, it's a process. It is long nights spent in prayer, agonizing times of passionate pursuit of the lost, and rejection by those around you. There's no magic formula that will allow you to forgo the struggles inherent to the Christian walk. To become a Christian capable of mightily impacting this world for Christ, we must be able to push past the emotions that would otherwise discourage us and shun anyone who would seek to extinguish our fire for God.

The bottom line is that this world needs us to be Christians who are prayer warriors driven by God's purposes, living in the power of the Divine, choosing purity over pleasure, living with a biblical perception of the existence and eternal ramifications of both heaven and hell, passionately pursuing Christ, propelled beyond the limitations of our comfort zones, and persistently and relentlessly striving to walk with God and impact the world with the life-saving Gospel of Jesus Christ!

By now we've been reminded that you and I are called to be far more than simple pew warmers taking up space once a week in our local church. Indeed, God has a major role for each of us in the grand scheme of building His eternal Kingdom. There is so much at stake; the eternal destiny of men, women, and children depend upon us fulfilling the Great Commission. The godly heritage that our forefathers fought, bled, and died to preserve is on the brink of disappearing forever. We've kicked God out of our public schools, the public square, and sadly, many of our homes too. As the times grow darker and darker, the bell towers of the church houses should be tolling day and night, rallying the saints together to stand as God's Holy army against these forces of darkness.

I hope you've made the decision to press the mute button on that small, nagging voice deep inside you that keeps saying things like, "Someone else will do it. It's a busy time in my life right now. I'll stand up and step out for Christ later.", or, "I'm not a preacher or a teacher, so I can't possibly make a difference." These are just a few of dozens of purpose-defeating thoughts that have likely been dominating your heart and mind for years. Make no mistake about it: Your flesh and the devil do not want you living for Christ outside of the four walls of your church, and they will do anything they can to stop you from becoming an active part of the Body of Christ.

Let's cut to the chase and expose these excuses for what they truly are: Dirty, stinking, filthy, crippling lies of the enemy intended to quench the fire that God has stoked in your heart. Don't be like the vast majority of ineffective Christians today who let the flesh get the best of them. The church, that's you and I, are promised that "the gates of hell shall not prevail against it." (Matthew 16:18) In other words, we've been assured of victory, and the only thing that can bring defeat is if we foolishly opt out of the fight. If we lose the victory now, it is only because we handed it to the enemy.

So, what exactly are you waiting for? The time has come for us to stop making lame excuses and looking for scapegoats and justifications for our lackadaisical approach to the Christian life. It's long past time that we took a stand for Christ, impacted the world, saved the lost, and defeated hell. It is my fervent hope that the Holy Ghost has gripped your heart and is urging you to become more dedicated to Christ than you've ever been before.

Christian brother or sister, can you hear the cry of the lost?

## THE CRY OF THE LOST

Do you hear the cry of the lost
Who for eternity will pay the cost?
Suffering torments they cannot tell
In the everlasting fire -- called Hell!

There they dwell where the worm dieth not
And relief can never be sought.
Eternal flames around them 'bout
Such horrid screams, can you hear them
shout?

It's too late! It's too late! For me,
But please dear Jesus, set my loved ones free.
Oh, tell them of your saving Grace
So they won't come to this wicked place.

Send someone to warn with tears
Of this place worse than all their fears.
To point them to the Savior above
And tell them of Your eternal love.

Prepare a man to be sent
And compel them to repent,
From all their guilt, sin, and strife
That they may have eternal life.

- ***James A. Kelly, III***

My friend, I pray that you won't be able to put this book out of your mind, and I hope that these truths will permeate your heart and spur you to action. We cannot silence the voice of the Savior as He pleads with us to share our faith with the world, and we surely will not silence the words of the saints who have gone before us, urging us to live for something far greater than ourselves.

Oh, my friend, if ever your soul has been persuaded to awaken from slumber, let it be now! If ever there was a time that you contemplated eternity and pondered leaping the chasm from hell to heaven, jump now! If ever your heart was broken by the guilt of complacency, may it be shattered now! If ever there was a time when the desperate pleas of the lost convicted our hearts, be convicted now! If ever there was a sense of urgency, a passion, and a will to stand and fight, let those passions consume us, and please Lord, let it happen today!

*"You may choose to look the other way but you can never say again that you did not know."*
*— William Wilberforce*

# ABOUT THE AUTHOR

Christian author and revivalist Josiah Martin is an inspirational speaker born and raised in Wooster, Ohio. Saved at the age of fourteen, he was called into full-time Christian service and began his preaching ministry at the age of fifteen.

Josiah has served as a full-time missionary with Rock of Ages Prison Ministry where he ministered to thousands of inmates and saw many men come to Christ. He currently serves as the youth pastor of GODSWORD Bible Church in Big Prairie, Ohio. Being burdened for the Church in America, the Lord has laid it upon Josiah's heart to encourage, exhort, and serve as a catalyst for revival in America.

Josiah's passionate, bold, and engaging delivery style is reminiscent of the fiery revivalists that have ushered in the world's previous great revivals. He is driven by a powerful and unquenchable passion to see Christians of all ages experience the life-changing power of Jesus Christ .

Josiah is a staunch believer that genuine, heaven-sent revival is the only hope for this country and indeed the entire world. It is his sincere desire to see the Holy Spirit of God sweep across this land once again!

Josiah is married to the love of his life, and best friend, Amy. They have one son, Kaleb. The Martins reside in Big Prairie, Ohio.

www.ingramcontent.com/pod-product-compliance
Lightning Source LLC
Chambersburg PA
CBHW070842050426
42452CB00011B/2378

* 9 7 8 1 9 4 3 4 9 6 0 0 6 *